0/100

THE GOSPEL TO THE SAINT

JIM VAN GELDEREN

THEEGENERATION
PUBLICATIONS

Copyright © 2019 by Thee Generation Publications.

Thee Generation Publications is a division of On To Victory Press, a ministry of Falls Baptist Church, N69W12703 Appleton Avenue, Menomonee Falls, WI 53051.

Thee Generation Publications is committed to providing written, digital, and audio resources to inspire a generation of young people to total surrender to God and total dependence on His power to reach the world with the gospel of Christ.

All Scripture quotations are taken from the King James Version, and out of respect, the author has purposely capitalized all personal pronouns referring to deity when quoting Scripture within the text.

Cover design by Bobby Bosler
Layout by Joe Mueller
Edited by Yvonne Sheppard
Special thanks to our proofreaders

The author and publication team have put forth every effort to give proper credit to quotes and thoughts that are not original with the author. It is not our intent to claim originality with any quote or thought that could not readily be tied to an original source.

All rights reserved. No part of this book may be reproduced, stored in a retrieval system, or transmitted in any form or by any means—electronic, mechanical, photocopy, recording, or otherwise—without written permission of the publisher, except for brief quotations in printed reviews.

ISBN: 978-1-951455-01-9
Printed in the United States of America

To my faithful wife, Rhonda,
who has walked with me as a patient
helpmeet in my 0/100 journey.

Contents

INTRODUCTION 7

CHAPTER 1
God's Theological Continental Divide 13

CHAPTER 2
Consideration #1: The Christian life is like salvation! 23

CHAPTER 3
Consideration #2: The Christian life is impossible! 33

CHAPTER 4
Consideration #3: The Christian life is spiritual! 41

CHAPTER 5
An Illustration of 0/100 51

CHAPTER 6
A Teenager's Story of 0/100 71

CHAPTER 7
My Beginning in 0/100 85

CONCLUSION 99

Introduction

"Faith is not a conclusion you reach . . . it's a journey you live."

A.W. Tozer

Introduction

I love the gospel, and I love teenagers. For the past 35-plus years, my wife and I have had the incredible privilege of traveling around the USA declaring the Good News of Jesus Christ to teenagers. I am stirred again and again as I see the Gospel to the Sinner impact lost teenagers. What a joy to see them enlightened with the simplicity of the glorious message of the gospel—Jesus saves! Sometimes this reality brings tears, other times a radiant smile, but no matter what the response, the wonderful reality that **Jesus has done it all** is the same! There is power in the message of the gospel!

However, there is another aspect of the gospel that I have also seen at work, powerfully impacting teens that already know the Lord. I call it the "Gospel to the Saint." You see, the gospel doesn't stop when you get saved; it's just getting started! This "Gospel to the Saint" is what this book is all about. There is good news for you as a believer: you don't have to live in defeat, powerlessness, and discouragement. You don't have to live a life of struggling to hold on, stay right, and hopefully make it to the end of the day without blowing it too badly. God never designed the Christian life to be that way, but that's where many of us live. If that's you, then you need the truth presented in this book.

What you need is a "paradigm shift"—a change in the way that you think about living the Christian life. I think you'll agree that every part of your life is directly affected by how you think. When you do not think biblically, you will experience negative effects in your life. The more significant the erroneous thinking, the more significant the adverse consequences. This is certainly true in the Christian life: thinking that includes any measure of self-dependence regarding the Christian life (unbiblical thinking) is destined to lead to a defeated Christian life in certain respects. That is why we need a biblical understanding of the concept of 0/100.

This book may not answer every question, and it may not make a specific application to every possible area of life, but I trust it will help you to start thinking about your Christian life in a whole new way. God intends for your Christian life to be victorious, restful, free, joyful, powerful, optimistic . . . and so much more! This kind of life doesn't happen by your working harder or putting in more sincere effort. It happens as you learn to walk in total surrender to God and total dependence on His power. We call this "sanctification by faith." It is the Gospel to the Saint, and that is what 0/100 is all about!

Chapter 1

GOD'S THEOLOGICAL CONTINENTAL DIVIDE

"Get to the end of yourself where you can do nothing, but where He does everything."

Oswald Chambers

Chapter 1

GOD'S THEOLOGICAL CONTINENTAL DIVIDE

I love driving my RV. Almost every Saturday, I jump into my F-350 dually with my fresh cup of Dunkin' coffee and head to our next meeting. Every three years or so we have a tour out West. While I love the rugged beauty of the West, sometimes towing an RV through the mountainous terrain can be quite a challenge. As I hit the Rocky Mountains, I cross over the foothills, traverse the first few mountain passes, and then I hit "The Big One"—a major mountain pass that tests my truck's pulling capacity. I tow a fairly heavy RV, so I can easily tell when I'm going uphill. I downshift to fourth gear, then third, and hopefully not second, as I labor for several miles up the steep incline to the top of the mountain. It's slow going, but I know I'm finally there when I see this sign, "United States Western Continental Divide." You see, this is no ordinary mountain top . . . that sign marks a line of great significance. If a raindrop falls on the eastern side of the Continental Divide, in theory it ends up in the Gulf of Mexico. If it falls on the western side of the Continental Divide, in theory it ends up in the Pacific Ocean. That's a big difference! Though those two raindrops might fall literally inches apart, their final destination is dramatically different.

In salvation, there is also a "continental divide." Perhaps we should call it a theological continental divide. If you choose the correct side of this theological divide, when you die, you end up going to heaven. If you choose the wrong side of the divide, you end up dying in your sins and going to an awful place that Jesus called hell. What an unbelievable difference! True Christians understand this divide . . . we realize that there's a difference between salvation by works and salvation by faith. One is a false gospel, and one is the true gospel.

However, when it comes to the theological continental divide in sanctification (the Christian life), Christians often miss the significant difference it can make. If you fall on the right side of the continental divide, you end up with victory, divine optimism, joy, blessing, and fruit in your life. If you fall on the wrong side of the divide, you end up frustrated, pessimistic, discouraged, and defeated.

So, you may ask . . . what is this theological continental divide? Perhaps this story will begin to explain. Several years ago, I was conducting a revival meeting in a church out West. I believe it was Wednesday night, and I was preaching an aspect of the truth that I am presenting here in this book. After the service, a young lady approached me. I'm guessing she was in her early 20s, and in a very thoughtful and sincere way she said, "Brother Van Gelderen, I have never heard what you preached tonight." To be honest, I initially wasn't sure how to take her statement, but she continued. "I grew up at such and such Baptist Church," she said, naming a significant independent Baptist church. "I moved out here a year ago. I have never heard what

0/100: THE GOSPEL TO THE SAINT

you preached tonight. I always thought the Christian life was 50/50—50% God and 50% me."

That is the divide—what you believe about how much of the Christian life is God's working, and how much is your working. Is it 50% God, and 50% you? Is it 60% God, 40% you? Is it 70/30? 80/20? 90/10? How about 95/5? What exactly **is** the Christian life? How much of it is you and how much of it is God? Your answer to that simple question determines which side of the continental divide you are on and therefore where your Christian life will end up, in victory or defeat.

STRIVING ACCORDING TO HIS WORKING

Even the mystery which hath been hid from ages and from generations, but now is made manifest to his saints: To whom God would make known what is the riches of the glory of this mystery among the Gentiles; which is Christ in you, the hope of glory: Whom we preach, warning every man, and teaching every man in all wisdom; that we may present every man perfect in Christ Jesus: Whereunto I also labour, striving according to his working, which worketh in me mightily.

– Colossians 1:26-29

GOD'S THEOLOGICAL CONTINENTAL DIVIDE

We find this theological divide addressed at the end of the first chapter of Colossians as the Apostle Paul declares a truth that had been hidden for ages but had now been revealed to believers. It was the great truth of "Christ in you." It is hard for us as New Testament believers to fully understand the shock that the idea of Deity's living within man would have brought. In the Old Testament times, only one person could experience the presence of God by going into the Holy of Holies, and he could go in only once a year. Even then, he had to go in the right way, or he would die! This is no longer the case. You have been given something far better . . . Christ in you! Think about it. The presence of God—the Shekinah Glory—is now in you. What a stunning reality of the finished work of Christ!

It was this amazing truth that Paul preached, taught, and warned of to the believers there at Colosse, knowing that it was the key to their being made "perfect [mature] in Christ Jesus." Not only that, but this truth was the foundation upon which Paul himself built his approach to ministry and the Christian life.

He lays out this approach in verse 29: "Whereunto I also labor, striving according to His working, which worketh in me mightily." What does Paul mean by that? Clearly he was laboring . . . he was striving . . . but was it according to his own strength? No. He was laboring "according to His working, which worketh in me mightily." So in Paul's Christian experience, how much was Paul and how much was God? Or, to bring it into the present, how much is you, and how much is God? Your answer to this question determines which side of the divide you fall on.

Perhaps you're wondering which side of the divide you are on right now. Ask yourself, "What kind of Christian life am I living?" Is it characterized by defeat, few answers to prayer, spiritual pessimism, discouragement, or powerlessness? Then perhaps you are on the wrong side of God's continental divide. But you don't have to stay there! God wants you to live on the right side of the divide and experience a life of regular answers to prayer, victories, encouragement, divine optimism, and supernatural power!

GOD'S THEOLOGICAL CONTINENTAL DIVIDE

You're probably thinking, "That sounds great, but how do I get on the right side of the divide?" The pathway is found in the answer to the initial question—how much of the Christian life is me and how much is God? Let's begin to do some simple searching of the Scriptures to discover the answer!

Chapter 2

CONSIDERATION #1: THE CHRISTIAN LIFE IS LIKE SALVATION!

"We are to walk in Christ the same way we originally received Christ—by faith."

Warren Wiersbe

Chapter 2

CONSIDERATION #1: THE CHRISTIAN LIFE IS LIKE SALVATION!

As a junior in college, I had a deep desire for God to use my life. I knew I was called to preach and had seen occasional blessing in my ministry, but overall, I was dry. I knew I needed something more, so each night I would leave the dormitory between 9:30 and 10:00 before dorm devotions with one goal in mind—to find God. It was my time to seek Him. I remember looking up into the starlit sky and saying, "God, where are you?" God heard the cry of my heart and answered by leading me to the biography of Hudson Taylor. Through the testimony of Taylor's life, a key truth began to slowly dawn on me—sanctification is by faith; it is not by works! That simple realization has literally changed my life.

THE CLARIFYING PRINCIPLE

As ye have therefore received Christ Jesus the Lord, so walk ye in him. — Colossians 2:6

In Colossians 2:6, we find the truth of sanctification by faith presented in simple terms that help us answer the key question, "How much of the Christian life is God and how much of the Christian life is me?" Read those words again: "As ye have therefore received Christ Jesus the Lord, so walk ye in Him." Fourteen simple words. In those words, however, I believe the Lord gives us a key principle of interpretation regarding sanctification. Note first of all that the phrase "received Christ Jesus the Lord" clearly refers to salvation, and "so walk ye in Him" refers to what we call "sanctification" in theology, or the Christian life. Adjacent to these phrases are the small words, "as" and "so," which reveal to us that there is a direct

CONSIDERATION #1: THE CHRISTIAN LIFE IS LIKE SALVATION

comparison to be made between salvation and the Christian life.

That doesn't mean that salvation and sanctification are without key differences. Clearly the goal of salvation is different than that of sanctification (the Christian life). The goal of salvation is to deliver us from the penalty of sin—eternity in hell. The goal of sanctification is to deliver us from the power of sin —defeat and bondage in our lives.

There is also a difference in the type of action being described. Salvation is an event that occurs in a moment of time; and once received, salvation is settled forever. Sanctification, however, is a process needing a constant supply of grace throughout the life of a believer. We see this difference clearly in the Greek verb tenses used here in Colossians 2:6. The word "received" is in a tense called the aorist tense, which views the action taking place as a whole, or as an event. Salvation is not a process; it is an event. While there might be a process that leads someone to salvation (emptiness, conviction, illumination, etc.), salvation itself occurs in a moment, when somebody who is lost and hell-bound trusts Jesus to do for them what they could never do for themselves, and He saves them. I like to call it "the salvation moment."

The verb "walk," however, is not in the aorist tense, but rather in the present tense. This is a distinct contrast, since the present tense communicates continuing action, or a process, rather than an event. So "walking in Him" is a process—a process that begins the moment a person is saved and continues until the moment they go home to heaven. It is a process that needs continual strength from God to be accomplished. It was this aspect of sanctification that inspired Major D.W. Whittle to pen the words, "Moment by moment, I've life from above," or as Lina Sandell put it, "Day by day and with each passing moment, Strength I find...." It is this process of sanctification that 0/100 is all about.

While it is crucial to understand these differences, they are not the primary point of Colossians 2:6. Paul was not trying to point out that salvation and sanctification are different; he wanted us to see that there is something about them that is **the same**. That

CONSIDERATION #1: THE CHRISTIAN LIFE IS LIKE SALVATION

is the truth that the Holy Spirit is communicating to us here in this verse. In other words, there is something that occurs in the moment of salvation ("As ye have therefore received Christ Jesus the Lord") that needs to be duplicated in every step of the Christian life ("so walk ye in Him"). Simply put, we can learn how to live the Christian life by looking at the key dynamic at work during the salvation moment.

What dynamic am I referring to? Think about this question: when you got saved, how much of the saving did Jesus do? All of it, right? We could say, "100%." Then how much of the saving did you do? None of it, or 0%, right? I don't say this to be unkind, but if your salvation depended on you just 1/100th of 1%, you would die in your sins and go to hell, because salvation is 0/100. There is absolutely nothing you can do to earn salvation. You have no ability to save yourself. You have only one hope: to come to God as a sinner, and—don't miss this—**trust Jesus** to do what you could never do. You can't wash your sins away. You can't make yourself righteous in the sight of God. You can't keep yourself out of hell, and you certainly can't give

29

yourself eternal life. But Jesus **can** do all of those things! You are a bankrupt sinner, but the moment you trust Jesus to do the saving that you can't do, He does it!

I'm guessing that by now you are probably thinking, "I think I get where this guy is going—if receiving salvation is 0/100, the walk of sanctification must be 0/100 too." I wish you could see me in your mind's eye at this moment, shouting an emphatic, "YES!" Look again at the "0" part of the equation. How much self-dependence does it take to keep someone from being saved? You know the answer . . . **any amount**! Imagine you were giving the gospel to your next-door neighbor and at the conclusion of your gospel presentation, they said, "I'm going to try as hard as I can to get saved. Maybe I can do five or ten percent of the saving, and trust Jesus to do the rest." Would you be excited? No, because you understand that partial dependence on self means there is only partial dependence on Jesus, and therefore, no salvation. Remembering the principle of Colossians 2:6, what if we move this same line of thinking to

CONSIDERATION #1: THE CHRISTIAN LIFE IS LIKE SALVATION

the Christian life? Imagine you are challenging a Christian friend about living the Christian life, and as you finish up, they say, "I'm going to work as hard as I can to live the Christian life and trust Jesus to do the rest." Would you be glad? You **shouldn't** be! I realize that might seem jarring, but please understand: just as in salvation, their partial self-dependence means they are not completely depending on Jesus, and they will, therefore, eventually end up in defeat. To summarize, let me ask it this way: how much self-dependence does it take in the Christian life before you are destined for defeat? And the answer is . . . **any amount**!

"Wait a minute!" you might say. "How does this line up with what we saw in Colossians 1:29? Wasn't Paul laboring? It says he was striving, right?" Yes, he **was** working. Certainly, he was laboring and striving. I can almost see him in my mind, wiping away the sweat pouring down his face as he walked through a day of serving the Lord. But how does that reconcile with 0/100? We're going to find that out, but first, we must understand Consideration #2.

Chapter 3

CONSIDERATION #2: THE CHRISTIAN LIFE IS IMPOSSIBLE!

"God doesn't expect the impossible from us. He wants us to expect the impossible from Him!"

Dwight L. Moody

Chapter 3

CONSIDERATION #2: THE CHRISTIAN LIFE IS IMPOSSIBLE!

A few years ago, I was preaching in a youth camp out West. Although I was the main speaker, the camp leadership had asked a dear young pastor to give a testimony. As he spoke, I was concerned as I heard him tell the teenagers, somewhat apologetically, "Teenagers, I know the Christian life is hard. I know the Christian life is difficult." I am sure he meant well, but I believe he got it completely wrong. I didn't want to embarrass him, but I felt like the wrong thinking needed to be corrected, so as I was preaching the next night, I declared, "Young people, the Christian life is not hard. The Christian life is not difficult. It's **impossible!**"

Do you understand how significant a difference that is? If the Christian life is just "hard" and "difficult," then what should you do when you are struggling in your Christian life? Try harder. Put in a little bit more effort. Grit your teeth just a bit longer. However, if the Christian life is not just difficult, but **impossible**, gritting your teeth and trying harder won't work. Putting in a little more effort won't make a difference. It's still impossible!

I realize that might sound a bit extreme initially, but I think the following questions will help to clarify what I'm saying. How much of the Bible can you be spiritually impacted by without the Holy Spirit? The answer is—none. How much effective praying can you do without the Holy Spirit? The answer is—none. How many people can you win to the Lord without the Holy Spirit? The answer is—none. How many other believers can we spiritually edify and encourage without the Holy Spirit? Again, the answer is—none. By now, you're probably seeing a pattern, right? Consider this last question carefully. How much true victory can you have without the Holy Spirit? Did you

CONSIDERATION #2: THE CHRISTIAN LIFE IS IMPOSSIBLE

hesitate on that one? Does the answer seem less cut and dry? Why? I think it is because of something that I call "false victory." There are times when you convince yourself that you're having victory, but you really aren't. False victory would be the lady who reports to her pastor, "Preacher, my husband did it to me again. He pushed every button I have, but I just clenched my teeth and didn't say a word. I thought of a million sarcastic things, but I didn't say even one of them. I had victory!" While her silence would certainly be better than her saying the things she would usually say, I wouldn't call that "victory" in the Bible sense. She has true victory when her husband pushes her buttons, and not only does she not **say** anything she shouldn't, but she doesn't even **want** to! I know what you're thinking—"That's impossible!" To which I say, "That's the whole point!"

So, back to the question—how much true victory can you have without the Holy Spirit? The answer is still . . . **none**. Please get this! The Christian life is not hard, it's not difficult . . . it's impossible! That's actually exciting! Think about it. If the Christian life is hard and difficult, then doing better means you need to try harder, to gut it out a little bit longer . . . it's all about you. But if it is impossible, then you need supernatural intervention, which means it's all about God—and with God, **nothing** is impossible. That gives us hope!

NOTHING REALLY MEANS NOTHING

I am the vine, ye are the branches: He that abideth in me, and I in him, the same bringeth forth much fruit: for without me ye can do nothing. – John 15:5

The night before His crucifixion, Jesus taught His disciples essential truths to prepare them for life after His departure. We find this instruction recorded in John 14-17. In John 15, Jesus uses the beautiful illustration of a grape vine's bearing fruit to explain several key aspects of the life of a disciple. In the middle of this illustration, however, we find a warning: "Without Me, ye can do nothing." Did you catch that? How much can you do without Jesus? Nothing! That may be shocking. It may even seem offensive. But

CONSIDERATION #2: THE CHRISTIAN LIFE IS IMPOSSIBLE

when Jesus says, "Without Me ye can do nothing," He means it—"nothing" really means nothing! The problem is that most of us don't seem to believe that. We think there are some things that we can do in our own strength, at least to some measure, and that is why we fail again and again. And when we fail, we get up and think, "I'm just going to have to try a little harder next time," missing the very point that God was trying to show us by allowing us to fail—we can't do it. **It's impossible**!

I remember one of those nights as a young preacher boy when I walked out under the night sky to seek God. In agony, I cried out in my heart, "God, I can't do this. God, I'm trying so hard; I can't do this, God, I just can't do it!" I honestly thought it was over for me. I probably couldn't have put it into words at the time, but I felt like God must have been up in heaven, wringing His hands and thinking, "Oh no, I'm about to lose another preacher boy." But I am confident today that God was not wringing His hands. If God was doing anything in heaven at that moment, He was saying, "It's about time you learned that you can't do it. Now we can get somewhere!" You see, "Without Me, ye can do nothing" really means exactly what it says—you can't do anything without Him. Major Ian Thomas, a man of God who understood this truth well, put it this way, "Why was Hudson Taylor what he was, and how could he do what he did? Why was A.B. Simpson what he was, and how could he do what he did? Were they God's favorites? Of course they were not! They were simply men who had qualified in the school of failure and despair. They were men who came to the end of themselves and discovered that what they were apart from God was nothing!"

If you and I can do nothing without Him, that means that living the Christian life is truly **impossible** without divine intervention. In other words, it is 0/100—nothing of us, and all of Him. Then what is the solution for us? We'll examine that as we look at Consideration #3 in the next chapter.

Chapter 4

CONSIDERATION #3: THE CHRISTIAN LIFE IS SPIRITUAL!

"When a man has no strength, if he leans on God, he becomes powerful."

Dwight L. Moody

Chapter 4

CONSIDERATION #3: THE CHRISTIAN LIFE IS SPIRITUAL!

"Why don't you pray for the people?" the young Chicago pastor responded, clearly troubled as two elderly ladies in his congregation told him they were praying for him. The Spirit-filled ladies replied with conviction, "Because **you** need the power of the Spirit." Though he was a good man, it was clear to these godly saints that their pastor lacked something spiritually. A short time later the young preacher was traveling with some friends to California. His heart was heavy with the reality of his own spiritual need, so he left his friends and went to another train car where he could be alone to cry out to God. You can almost hear the agony in his spirit as you read the words of his prayer, as told by his biographer, Richard Ellsworth Day. "Oh God have mercy! There is something wrong with me! In His dear Name, correct me! I'd rather die than go on this way." Just a simple cry of desperation, but in that moment, D. L. Moody began to understand a life-changing truth—he was not just weak: he had absolutely **no** spiritual strength without God! This was not the end of D. L. Moody. Far from it—it was just the beginning! This key understanding transformed his life in a remarkable way, eventually sending him around the world in dynamic ministry touched by the reviving presence of God.

D. L. Moody was not an isolated individual who needed God more than most. We are all in the same desperate condition: in ourselves, we have absolutely no spiritual strength. This is not to say that we don't have **physical** strength. We do. You are holding this book in your hand right now, reading it, and using your brain to think about it. You are using physical muscles. If you weren't, you would be dead! But victory in your Christian life requires more than just physical strength; it requires **spiritual** strength, because it is

CONSIDERATION #3: THE CHRISTIAN LIFE IS SPIRITUAL

spiritual growth that needs to take place. This is the reason that the Christian life is impossible, as we saw in the last chapter—we have absolutely no spiritual strength, which is what we need in order to live the Christian life.

Jesus' words in II Corinthians 12:9 are His answer to the Apostle Paul's plea for God to take away his "thorn in the flesh," and they reflect the depth of spiritual need in our lives. He said, "My grace is sufficient for thee: for My strength is made perfect in **weakness**" [emphasis added]. The word translated "weakness" is a fascinating word in the Greek language; it is the word "strength" with an alpha, or an *a*, attached to the beginning. The addition of an alpha takes the meaning of the word and negates it, just as it does in the English language. For example, a "theist" is somebody who believes in God; but if you put an *a* before the word "theist," how does it change the definition? Radically, right? Instead of being somebody who believes in God, an atheist is the complete opposite—someone who doesn't believe in God at all! In the same manner, the word for "weakness" means, in the most basic sense, "no strength."

This meaning of the word "weakness" is echoed in the *Theological Dictionary of the New Testament*, where one of the definitions listed is "'impotence' in the sense of 'inner poverty' or 'incapacity.'" *Strong's Concordance* also supports this definition, stating that "weakness" comes from the word which means "strengthless . . . without strength."

I realize that this is different from what we usually mean when we use the word "weakness." We usually mean that we aren't feeling quite up to the task, or that we don't have quite enough strength. But that is not what the word means in the context of our spiritual life. "Weakness" is the complete absence of strength—no strength at all. Do you see the significance of this distinction? If you are weak, how much spiritual strength do you have without Jesus? Though it might be hard to admit, you don't have "just a little" strength. You don't even have "barely any" strength. You have **no** spiritual strength! In other words, you are completely bankrupt of spiritual strength.

CONSIDERATION #3: THE CHRISTIAN LIFE IS SPIRITUAL

Isn't that exciting? It might not seem that way at first, but let the truth sink in. Jesus said, "My strength is made perfect in weakness." The phrase "made perfect" means to be completed, fulfilled, or finished. So, it is in the situations where you realize that you have absolutely no strength that Jesus has the opportunity to fully display His supernatural strength in your life. That is why Paul went on to say, "Most gladly therefore will I rather glory in my infirmities, that the power of Christ may rest upon me." The word translated as "infirmities" is actually the same word as "weakness"; it is just plural instead of singular. In other words, the "infirmities" are "strengthlessnesses," or areas in which you have absolutely no strength. In the face of this utter lack of strength, Paul decided that he wouldn't just cope with it—he would rejoice in it! It's almost as if Paul were throwing his sandals into the air and exclaiming, "I'm weak! I'm weak! Hallelujah! I have no strength at all!" Why? Because he came to understand that his utter lack of spiritual strength was the key to the "power of Christ" resting on him.

You can find our complete lack of spiritual strength reflected in other passages as well. Consider Ephesians 6:10: "Be strong in the Lord, and in the power of His might." We are commanded, "Be strong," but is it in our own might? No. It is "in the power of **His** might" [emphasis added]. This reality is also found in the oft-quoted words of Philippians 4:13, where Paul says, "I can do all things through **Christ** which strengtheneth me" [emphasis added]. These words are so familiar that we can easily overlook the whole point. Whose strength is it? Not ours, but Christ's!

The message of the Word of God is clear: in ourselves we don't have any spiritual strength. As I look back on the early days of my Christian life, I remember thinking, "I'm going to get stronger and stronger as a Christian, and certainly by the time I'm 50 I'll be a strong Christian." Now that I'm over 50 years old, I realize that I still have problems . . . I'm still weak! Though I've certainly grown and matured, I look at my life in a completely different way now. The Christian life is not "weak little me" getting stronger and stronger. Rather, the Christian life is

CONSIDERATION #3: THE CHRISTIAN LIFE IS SPIRITUAL

"weak little me," who always has been weak and always will be weak, tapping into the One who is strong and will always be strong. It is someone with no strength tapping into the supernatural strength of the omnipotent God of the universe. That is when the impossible becomes the possible—when it isn't your strength, but His!

I know what you are probably thinking—"Okay. I get it. I don't have any strength, but Jesus does. But how on earth do I live that out? How do I put it into practice in my home, my school, or my workplace?" I hope to begin to answer those questions in the next chapter, as we look at a biblical illustration that sheds light on what 0/100 looks like in real life.

Chapter 5

AN ILLUSTRATION OF 0/100

"Complete weakness and dependence will always be the occasion for the Spirit of God to manifest His power."

Oswald Chambers

Chapter 5

AN ILLUSTRATION OF 0/100

The day had finally come! The 15-year-old boy had eagerly anticipated his 16th birthday, and now the wait was finally over. He replayed the words of his father in his mind again and again: "Son, I walked on water on my 16th birthday. My dad walked on water on his 16th birthday, and my grandfather walked on water on his 16th birthday." Now it was time for him to put his legacy to the test. He persuaded a friend to row him out to the middle of a nearby lake. Taking a deep breath, he stepped out onto the surface of the water, fully expecting that he, like his father, would walk on water. His high hopes were dashed as . . . blub, blub, blub . . . he came up gasping for air. Climbing back into the boat, his friend helped him back to the shore where the drenched and humbled boy went to find his father. "Dad," he asked, as he approached his father, "You walked on water on your 16th birthday. Your dad walked on water on his 16th birthday. Your grandfather walked on water on his 16th birthday. Why couldn't I?" His father replied with a twinkle in his eye, "Son, our birthdays were in January. Yours is in June!"

We chuckle at this story, because we all know that walking on water (in its liquid form) isn't just difficult. It's impossible! You could train for 20 years to walk on water, but after all that training, you'd still be no closer to doing it than when you began. We have many skilled athletes in America, but no matter how strong or capable they are, not a single one can walk on water, because **it's impossible**. That means that nobody has ever done it, right? Wrong! It has been done, even though it is impossible.

GET OUT OF THE BOAT

If you have even a casual knowledge of the Bible, you probably know that there are two people who have walked on water—Jesus and Peter. "Yes," you might say, "but Jesus is God. He can do anything." That is true. However, there was a human who was just like you and me in every way who also walked on water. You know his name: Peter. The account of Peter's walking on water is a tremendous help in understanding what the truth of 0/100 looks like in day-to-day life. Peter was an ordinary guy who made a lot of mistakes, yet he walked on water. If God could supernaturally empower Peter to do the impossible, then He can do the same for you and me. The question is, "How?"

The scene in the boat opens in Matthew 14 with the disciples "in the midst of the sea" of Galilee. Now, the Sea of Galilee is about 8 miles wide and 13 miles long, so to be "in the midst of the sea" means they were about 4 miles from the closest shore. That's a long way! In addition, they were being "tossed with waves" because "the wind was contrary." They were caught out on the water in the middle of a violent storm that was threatening their lives. No doubt their oil lamps had been blown out long ago, and the stormy sky was hiding the light of the moon. They fought through the storm for most of the night, finding no relief until "in the fourth watch of the night Jesus went unto them, walking on the sea." The fourth watch of the night is the time from 3:00 to 6:00 in the morning. Since the disciples were able to see Jesus, I think it was probably closer to 6:00, and the dim, gray light of the stormy dawn was giving them just enough light to catch a glimpse of the figure of a man walking towards them on the white-capped waves.

Can you imagine the shock they must have felt? It's no wonder that "they cried out for fear"! They thought Jesus was an apparition—a spirit—until He spoke those assuring words of comfort, "It is I; be not afraid." Hearing those words, Peter cried out through the howling wind and crashing waves, "Lord, if it be Thou, bid me come unto Thee on the water." This "if" statement is called a first-class condition, which means that the "if" statement is assumed to be true.

In other words, Peter wasn't saying, "Lord, it might be You, but it might not be. Prove to me it is really You." Rather, what Peter was saying was, "Lord, I know it's You, and since it's You, tell me to come to You on the water." Jesus uttered one word in response to Peter's request—"Come."

Let's pause the story there for just a moment to ask two key questions that help us grasp what is happening and to come to the right conclusions. When Peter got out of the boat to go to Jesus, did he use his muscles, his physical strength? Yes, of course he did. He had to move actual muscles and use physical strength to get out of the boat. But here is the crucial question: was he trusting his muscles and physical strength to walk on the water? I think the answer is clear—no, not at all!

Do you get it? The Christian life is "getting out of the boat." It is not just obeying Jesus, but it's depending on Jesus to enable you to do what you could never do unless He enabled you to do it. It is not passivity; it is His spiritual strength empowering you to do what you could never do unless Jesus supernaturally empowered you to do it! In other words, Jesus didn't walk over to the boat, grab Peter, and pull him out onto the water. Peter had to obey Jesus by using his muscles, but he wasn't trusting his muscles to keep him afloat; he was trusting Jesus! Major Ian Thomas articulates this truth beautifully in his classic book, *The Indwelling Life of Christ*, where he says, "To 'let go and to let God' is not inactivity, but Christ-activity— God in action accomplishing divine purposes through human personality." Friend, it is not passivity; it is His activity through you!

MAKING IT PRACTICAL

Let's take this perspective and apply it to a modern-day situation. When you go out soulwinning, you're going to use physical strength, right? You do have to move physical muscles in order to walk to the door, ring the doorbell, and then speak words; but the key to success in soulwinning has nothing to do with that. The key to fruitful soulwinning is trusting Jesus to spiritually strengthen you to do the impossible. I call this "dependent obedience." Anytime we give the gospel, it should be like getting out of the boat and saying, "Jesus, I'm depending on you to enable me to do what I can never do unless You enable me to do it." Only then can you "walk on water"!

I cannot remember where I heard it, but it has been said, "The average life of a soulwinner is seven years." Please understand—if that's true, it's not because soulwinners are getting gunned down at the front door. It is because they quit! Why? What could cause someone with a sincere heart for the lost to quit trying to reach them? Though there are a variety of factors, I believe the primary reason is this—they were on the wrong side of the theological continental divide. Though they were sincere, they had some measure of self-dependence, and **any** measure of self-dependence sets you up for failure. To put it simply, even 5/95 doesn't work; it must be 0/100.

But you don't have to live a life of self-dependence and failure. That is the glory of 0/100! When you're on the right side of the continental divide, you can know the thrill of "walking on water," just like Peter. Have you ever experienced that? Ask anyone who has trusted God in an impossible situation and seen His divine intervention, and they will confirm what I'm saying: it is thrilling when Jesus enables you to do what you know you cannot do!

Walking on water is an incredible experience, but you will never experience it unless you get out of the boat. If you're thinking, "I don't think I can give the gospel," or, "I'm too shy to go out soulwinning," you are the perfect candidate to see God work. Remember, Peter couldn't walk on water either, but he looked to Jesus and stepped out of the boat. Why don't you decide to show up for soulwinning, but before you go, cry out to Jesus, saying, "Jesus, I can't do this, but You can enable me to do this because it's Your will. I am trusting You completely, because I have no strength at all." Then go out, moving your physical muscles but depending solely on Jesus to enable you to do it, and watch God enable you to "walk on water"!

Now, you need 0/100 in every area of your life, not just in soulwinning. What does 0/100 look like when we talk about dealing with hidden sin? Consider the teenager fighting against the Holy Spirit's conviction about hiding sin from their parents. I've lost track of how many times I've heard the words, "I could never tell my parents what I've done!" That statement is usually followed by a multitude of reasons why, but regardless of the reasons, the answer is the same—if it is God's will, you can do it through His strength. Yes, you have to take the step to "get out of the boat" by moving your lips and talking, but if you're trusting Jesus, He will give you the power to do what seems impossible to you right now.

Several years ago, a young man came to a youth conference where I was preaching. His parents had bought him the plane ticket to come, so even though he did not want to come, he knew he had to attend. During the conference his younger brother got right with the Lord. As his brother stood and testified of what God had done in his heart, the older brother knew he needed to do the same. It seemed impossible, but he knew that he had to tell his dad all the shameful things he had being doing in secret. When he got home, he "got out of the boat" and asked his dad if they could talk. They went on a walk, stopping at a park bench where they sat down as the young man began to reveal everything he had been doing. He testified later that the moment he began to tell his dad everything, God strengthened him, enabling him to go all the way. His younger brother shared a similar testimony.

How about you? Perhaps you need to uncover some sin you have been hiding to someone who deserves to know. For a teenager who cheated on his schoolwork, that may be a teacher or a principal. For an employee that didn't follow the company guidelines, that could be an employer. For a son or daughter that did things behind their parent's back, it could be that parent they deceived. I realize that going to the appropriate person to confess your sin is intimidating; that is why you will need to trust the Lord for the spiritual strength as you take the step to begin an uncomfortable conversation. I have heard testimonies of hundreds who did this and found freedom!

> "I've a joy and a peace after apologizing to my parents and [uncovering] the stuff I've hidden from them."

"So for a while now, I've been struggling with something. I've . . . been hiding it behind my parents' back. And this week's messages . . . they just really convicted me and I was able to go back and tell a counselor about my situation. And I got it right with my parents. And I've been set free."

"But you don't know what I've done. I don't think 0/100 could get me out of this." No matter what sinful choices you have made, or how deeply that sin has embedded itself into your daily life, there is true hope, because the victory has nothing to do with your ability to free yourself. Though getting out of the mess you've created seems impossible, Jesus **will** free you as you trust Him to do what you cannot do. It just starts with your taking the first step. Get out of the boat!

Maybe you aren't hiding sin in your life, but your Christian life just seems dull and meaningless. You're going through the motions but lack any true reality of God. That's because you need 0/100 to have a vibrant, personal walk with God. I remember a young lady in a Christian school where our team was conducting the War of Special Forces. On the final night at our campfire service, she stood and shared this stirring testimony. "I have my devotions every day, but I have been getting nothing from them. At the beginning of the week, I asked the Lord, 'O God, will You show me why?' Yesterday, God showed me why. **I've** been trying to get something from my devotions. Yesterday I read a chapter and got nothing from it. Today I opened my Bible to the same chapter. This time I prayed, 'God, would You please teach me?'" Tears began to run down her face as she spoke the last words of her testimony, "Oh, today God showed me so many things."

Are you tired of duty-bound devotions? Do you want to actually hear from God? Next time you open your Bible, tell God you need Him to teach you because you can't understand His Word in your own strength, and then see what He will do. Get out of the boat!

There's just one problem, right? Getting out of the boat is scary! It certainly is if you are looking at how impossible the situation seems. That is why your eyes must be on Jesus. "But wait," you might be thinking, "if I get out of the boat, I'm going to do exactly what Peter did. I'm going to take a few steps, take my eyes off Jesus, and down I'll go." You're right. It's really not a question of **if** that's going to happen; it's a matter of **when**. We are all so prone to self-dependence that it doesn't take much to get our eyes back on ourselves instead of Jesus. You might be thinking, "If that's the case, I'd rather just play it safe and stay in the boat!" But do you remember what Peter did when he took his eyes off Jesus and began to sink beneath the waves? He cried out to Jesus in what I like to call a "flare-prayer." I'm not talking about the way Christians usually pray today—"Dear Jesus, thank you for this day . . . ." If Peter had prayed like that, it would have been, "Dear Jesus, thank you for blub-blub-blub-blub-blub." A "flare-prayer" is a passionate, quick, desperate cry sent heavenward because you are in deep need of deliverance. Peter prayed just three words—"Lord, save me!" Was it an effective prayer? Absolutely! Those three simple words of dependence on Jesus moved the heart of the Savior, and He saved Peter. He will save you too!

You see, that is what you need when things are impossible—a Savior. Perhaps the phrase we have heard spoken so often, "accepting Jesus Christ as your personal Savior," is so familiar to us that it has lost its meaning. Allow me to adjust the phrase slightly, using modern terminology to help what I'm saying come to life. I'm talking about your accepting Jesus Christ as your personal *lifeguard*, as your personal *fireman*, as your personal *EMT*, as your personal *rescue worker*. These terms accurately depict the role of a savior. A savior is a "rescuer," which is exactly what Jesus is for you and me. When you got saved, Jesus' rescue work wasn't done—it was just beginning! The first thing He rescued you from was the penalty of sin, but from the moment you got saved until the moment you die, He also wants to rescue you from the power of sin. That is who He is! No matter where you are or why you are sinking, the instant you look to Him to do what you realize you cannot do, He will rescue you!

OBEDIENCE & SURRENDER

I have been emphasizing the vital dynamic of total dependence on Jesus, but I would like to briefly clarify two other essential dynamics that are also in play as we "get out of the boat" in a life of 0/100. The first is obedience. Do you remember the last thing Jesus said before Peter got out of the boat? He said, "Come," right? Now, that simple word was not just an invitation to believe God for the impossible; it was also a command to take the step into the impossible. Because Peter was believing on Jesus, he obeyed Jesus. That is how 0/100 works! When you have total dependence on Jesus to enable you to do what you could never do, you obey! You're not looking for a feeling. You're not waiting for a lightning bolt from heaven. You just obey Jesus, believing that He will empower you to do what He commands you to do. You don't have to fear when you receive the commands of Jesus, because your Commander is also your Enabler—whatever He tells you to do, He will empower you to do as you trust in Him.

I don't think anyone has said it more clearly than the songwriter, John Sammis, when he wrote, "Trust and obey, for there's no other way to be happy in Jesus, but to trust and obey." If you say you are trusting God, yet you don't obey, do you know what that means?

You don't really trust God. This is what James was talking about when he wrote to Jewish believers and said, "Faith without works is dead." God wants you to realize that if you really believe that He will do what He says, you'll obey Him. That is 0/100—a life of God-dependent obedience, trusting God to do what you could never do unless He enabled you to do it.

The second essential dynamic that you need to understand is surrender. If you are going to trust and obey God, that means you must be willing to do what He is telling you to do. In other words, for there to be a total **dependence** on the Lord, there also must be total **surrender** to the Lord. Using our 0/100 terminology, the Christian life is 100% God's will and 0% your will. If you want to completely depend on God to obey, then you must completely surrender your will to His.

My brother John illustrates this truth with the picture of rowing a boat. If you have ever tried to row a boat with only one oar, you know that it is difficult to make much progress. You can be rowing with all your might, but what happens if you use only one oar on one side of the boat? You go in circles! You need both oars in the water, one on each side of the boat, in order to move forward. The two oars represent total surrender to the will of God and total dependence on God's grace to do it. You need both oars to make progress in your Christian life. If you say, "Lord, I've got some really good plans for my life. Please bless them and enable me to do what I want to do," it's not going to work! While you may have the "total dependence" oar in the water, you've rejected the "total surrender" oar. Imbalance in the other direction produces a similar result. You might say, "Lord, show me Your will and I will work as hard as I can to do it," but you still have only one oar in the water—the "total surrender" oar. Through your self-dependence, you have rejected the "total dependence" oar, and as a result, you will still be going in circles—a lot of activity but getting nowhere.

Well, friend . . . what area of your life is it that seems impossible? Is there an impossible step that Jesus is calling you to take in dependence upon Him? Don't hang back in fear and unbelief. Cry out to Jesus, submit to His will, and take that step. It's time to get out of the boat!

Chapter 6

A TEENAGER'S STORY OF 0/100

"God wants us to know that when we have Him, we have everything."

A.W. Tozer

Chapter 6

A TEENAGER'S STORY OF 0/100

In 2011, a 16-year-old teenager named Ryan Swanson came to College Day at Baptist College of Ministry in Menomonee Falls, Wisconsin. During the chapel service that day, I preached a message from Proverbs 29:25: "The fear of man bringeth a snare: but whoso putteth his trust in the LORD shall be safe." The crux of the message was this: if you trust God, you won't fear man; but if you fear man, you are not trusting God. God used that simple message to drive truth home in Ryan's heart. Though Ryan knew he should give the gospel, he had been bound by the fear of man . . . it just seemed impossible to talk to his co-workers about Jesus. Below is his own account of how God changed his life and the lives of those around him as he began to live out the truth of 0/100.

I always knew God wanted me to preach, but I also knew I couldn't do it. I was so terrified of public speaking that I refused even to discuss the possibility of preaching because of the deep, sickening anxiety that accompanied it. When I finally surrendered to God's will at fourteen-years-old, however, He gave me an excitement for His calling as an evangelist that never really went away. I knew I was still just as inadequate for the task, but I was excited about someday being an evangelist and someday being able to unashamedly give the gospel. I was certain I couldn't achieve this calling at that point in my life, but I assumed that after enough time at Bible college, I would suddenly be able to do what had always been impossible, and then I would begin ministry.

At the age of sixteen, I began working at a distribution center for a grocery chain called Hy-Vee.

It was an extensive facility with three warehouses, each of them nearly a quarter of a mile long and accommodating several hundred employees. I worked from 6 p.m. until 2 a.m., and because this shift was designed for students like myself, I was working with scores of other young people, five days a week. I spent a lot of time with those teens, but I'm sorry to say that in my first six months there, I hadn't once given the gospel.

In February, I took a few days off from work and joined my family in attending the Victory Conference at Falls Baptist Church and the College Day for Baptist College of Ministry. During the chapel service, Dr. Jim Van Gelderen preached a message titled "The Fear of Man." I can't tell you every verse he used or every point in his outline, but I can tell you that the Lord was all over me about one thing: Hy-Vee Distribution Center. Though I had surrendered my future calling to the Lord, my life since had not changed, because I had failed to trust Him for daily enabling. My plan was to build relationships that would lead to the gospel, but that wasn't working. My plan was to live a testimony that would lead to the gospel, but that hadn't worked either. My plan hadn't worked because my plan didn't require God. Building relationships and having a good testimony were things I could do in my own strength. Since I was still depending on my plan to do God's work, the same feeling of inadequacy that had initially kept me from the call to preach was now keeping me from experiencing God's deliverance in giving the gospel.

Dr. Jim's message came on a Friday, and I responded to the work God was doing in my heart. I committed to giving the gospel to a coworker the following night, although I didn't know how to go about it. I didn't think it would be right to give the gospel on company time, but who would want to listen to me after the shift ended at 2 a.m.? I didn't have a plan, but it was God's mission, and for the first time, I was depending on Him completely for both the plan and the ability.

I went to work at 6 p.m. Saturday night. A couple hours into the shift, something happened that had never happened before. My job at that warehouse consisted of loading boxes of food onto pallets, which would then be moved into refrigerated trailers for delivery. This night, however, the company ran out of those refrigerated trailers. I never figured out exactly why it happened that night, but it had never happened before, and it never happened again in my time working there. It became obvious to me fairly quickly that this was no accident. With no work to do, scores of employees stood around with nothing to do but talk and wait for further instruction from the managers. The Lord had set it up, and He enabled as I took the stack of tracts I had brought and began handing them out to groups of men and teenagers, offering to tell anyone how they could be sure of a home in heaven. Tim was a teenager who received a tract that night, though I gave it to him reluctantly. In the weeks prior, he had mocked me because he had found out I went to church. I was shocked by his response, however. He came to me later that night, thanked me for the tract, and promised to read it. The next time I saw Tim, he said, "I read that thing you gave me, and I memorized the prayer on the back." It was obvious that he hadn't understood everything he'd read in the tract, so I said, "Tim, if you want me to explain how you can have your sins forgiven and be on your way to heaven, then meet me after work tonight." At 2 a.m. I had my first gospel meeting after work. Tim stood listening for 45 minutes in the cold before he prayed and accepted Christ as his Savior. After that, Tim began faithfully coming to church and growing rapidly in the Lord. What I didn't know was that this was just the beginning of what God wanted to accomplish at Hy-Vee.

After Tim was Dominic, then Chase, and then Cole. Cole was known in the warehouse and in the community as being the "party kid," the underaged drinker. He and his older brother would invite guys of all ages over to their house, and they would party all night. It became a joke in the warehouse. I went to Cole that night, confident that he was the one whom the Lord was leading me to. I said, "Cole, I'm pretty sure that God wants me to give you the gospel tonight and tell you how you can know for sure that you're on your way to heaven." Cole quickly replied, "No man, I don't have time for that. I need to get home. I'm tired."

He wouldn't listen at all, but a bunch of his friends were standing around—Dominic, Chase, and another new Christian, Lane—almost all guys who had been saved there at the warehouse. They were telling him, "You need to listen to this guy. You need to get this." But Cole didn't want to hear it and reminded Lane, "You said you'd give me a ride home. Let's go." Lane simply replied, "No, I'm not going to take you home. Ryan's going to take you home, and he's going to tell you how to be saved on the way." Finally, Cole turned to me and said, "Look, Ryan, I'll go with you, but you have to drive the speed limit, and you've got to go the way I tell you. It's going to take 5 minutes, and if you want to talk to me in those 5 minutes, that's fine, but that's it." We got into my car and started off toward his house, but as soon as I pulled onto the road, a pickup truck sped past me, moved back over into our lane, and slowed down to 5 mph. It was a no-passing zone all the way to Cole's house, so there was nothing I could do about it. As it turned out, the driver of the pickup was Lane, who thought his friend could use a little more than 5 minutes to hear the gospel! I had

15-20 minutes in that drive to give Cole the gospel, and by the time we got to his house, he wouldn't let me stop. "You've got to finish! I've never heard this before!" Before that night was over, Cole called out to the Lord in his driveway and was saved.

After Cole were Tyler, Ed, and Pavel. Eventually, I would just walk into the parking lot after work, and I knew God would have someone there for me who was ready for the gospel. Every time was a miracle, and I knew He was going to do it as long as I was trusting in Him.

One night, as I came out of the warehouse, I remember being especially convinced that a soul would be saved. There was only one other guy in the parking lot, which normally would make it easy, but this was Jake. I never would have picked Jake out of a crowd to give him the gospel. He had about 10 years on me, was very cocky, and wouldn't give me the time of day in the warehouse. I would rather have tried to convert a squirrel in the parking lot, but I only saw Jake. I knew Jake wouldn't listen, but I also knew the Lord had promised me a soul, so I ran over to him. He didn't even turn to look at me when I reached him, so I just started in, "Hey Jake, I know this is going to sound odd, but I'm pretty sure God wants me to give you the gospel tonight and tell you how you can be 100% sure you're on your way to heaven." "No man, I don't got time for that," Jake mumbled as he kept walking towards his car. I kept following him and tried again, "Look man, this isn't me, this is God. He's wanting to tell you something tonight." By now we had reached his car, and without another word, he jumped in, slammed his door, and took off. There I was, left in the parking lot, confused. I knew God had wanted me to talk to Jake, and I had fully expected him to get saved that night.

I was shocked the following night when Jake walked up to me with a different look on his face. I had no idea what to expect. He began hesitantly, "Ryan, I need to talk to you. As soon as I left you last night, when you were trying to tell me about God, I got this really bad feeling. I knew I had said 'No' to God and something bad was going to happen. I knew I was going to get in a wreck. I knew it was the night I was going to hit a deer." Sure enough, as he was driving home that night, the biggest buck Jake had ever seen jumped out in front of him. He hit it so hard that the deer rolled up over the hood, breaking through the windshield. The head of the deer whipped around from the impact, and the antlers broke through the driver's side door at him. He should have been killed. There was this rough guy, who never would have talked about God before, saying to me, "Whatever you were going to tell me last night about God, I need to hear it!" Still in shock, I told him to meet me after work. We met in the parking lot at 2 a.m., I gave him the gospel, and he accepted Christ. Over and over this was happening—a new miracle every time.

Another night, I was out in the parking lot giving the gospel to two teenagers, while my brother was witnessing to another guy. All three had accepted Christ by 3 a.m. when the general manager of the warehouse walked out. It was rare to see him; he had been off work for weeks after a fall from his roof had nearly killed him, but even though he was back, our paths did not often cross. Immediately I knew that

God wanted me to give him the gospel. There I was, a young teenager running across the parking lot, waving down the manager at 3 a.m. He had just settled into his car, ready to close the door, when he saw me. "Wes," I said, "sometimes coming so close to death can really wake you up to your need for God. Can I tell you what God says about how to know for sure you're going to heaven?" He said, "Yeah, I need that." I knelt down beside his car and showed him from Scripture how to be saved. About 30 minutes later, he bowed his head and accepted Christ. Scenes like this continued to happen, and by the end of just two years of working at that warehouse before I left for college, there were 26 coworkers who had accepted Christ.

I never could have imagined all that God did in those two years. I wouldn't have even known to ask for what He did. To some, the Hy-Vee Distribution Center became known as the Hy-Vee Revival Center, but it wasn't because of me. You may think that I'm some special person or that I have some special gifting or personality, but if you knew me, you would know that's not the case. This is something that I still have to constantly surrender to the Lord. I feel that ever since that Friday session, when God changed my thinking and revealed my self-dependence, I find more self-dependence in my life every day. Though I'm now a graduate of Bible college and seminary, I'm still just as inadequate and just as ineffective without Christ. Ultimately, the resolve of total surrender and total dependence is practically seen in daily decisions. Every night at the warehouse was another battle with self, but each time Christ won in my heart, He also won in the warehouse. God's plans for you are bigger than you can imagine. If you'll commit to a life of total surrender and total dependence, you will see God use you in ways you never could have asked or thought. He wants to begin right now!

Chapter 7

MY BEGINNING IN 0/100

"Recognize that you are nothing
in yourself."

Wayne Van Gelderen, Sr.

Chapter 7

MY BEGINNING IN 0/100

Growing up, I was extremely shy. During my 6th grade year, my dad started a Christian school, where I attended for the rest of my school years. When I was in the 10th grade, my uncle came to preach at our Christian school. He had been paralyzed in a terrible car accident in his younger years, so he was preaching from a wheelchair. It was high school chapel, and there were about 250 students seated there in the auditorium. In front of all those people, my uncle looked at me and said, "Jimmy, [which is what they called me back then], read such-and-such passage of Scripture." I opened my Bible, but as I stood to my feet, I felt like there was a huge apple stuck in my throat. I could feel the heat rolling off of my face as I turned bright red. Somehow, I choked out the verses while tears began to well up in my eyes. As soon as I finished, I closed my Bible and sat down, thinking, "I hope **that** never happens again!"

When I was 16 years old, I found myself fighting a growing conviction that I was called to preach. Finally, at the end of that junior year, I couldn't push it off any longer. With deep conviction, I walked down the aisle of Marquette Manor Baptist Church, where my dad pastored, grabbed my dad's hand, and said, "Dad, I think God is calling me to preach." I will never forget my dad's response. It stunned me. He tenderly said, "Jim, your mother and I have known that for a long time; we've been praying for you." They had seen all along what God was doing, but I had had no clue.

"Well," you might say, "was the burden lifted? Were you excited?" Frankly, no—I wasn't excited at all. In fact, I was miserable, because I didn't believe I could do it. I stood out in the lobby after the service, thinking, "Okay, I've got my senior year of high school, freshman year of college, sophomore, junior, senior—

five years. Maybe something will happen!" I thought I still had five years before I had to do the thing I dreaded, preaching. But my dad didn't believe that. He believed that if you were called to preach, you should start doing it right away!

My dad was well known in the Chicago area at that time, so area pastors would often call him if they needed someone to fill their pulpit. "Dr. Van Gelderen," they would ask, "I am going to be out of town. Would you send a staff member over to fill the pulpit while I am gone?" My dad always agreed to send someone, but this time when he was asked, he didn't volunteer a staff member—he volunteered me! "My 16-year-old son just yielded to the call to preach—I'll send him over."

I remember that Sunday morning well. My dad sent me **alone**. I drove over to the inner-city church and parked my car outside the old building lined with stained glass windows. When I walked into the church, I felt like I had walked into a retirement home. Everyone in the room seemed old. The youngest person might have been in their 40s, but when you're

16 years old, somebody 40 years old has got one foot in the grave and is slipping fast! One thing was certain—I was the youngest person in the room. I took a moment to look over my outline, but all I could think was, "This is the sorriest thing I have ever seen."

The song service was pretty slow and dry, and then it was time for me to preach. After being introduced, I went to the pulpit and unfolded my outline. For 25 to 30 minutes, I labored through my notes, desperately trying to get to the end, while the thought flashed through my mind, "I thought the singing was dry, but this is worse!" By the time I finally finished, I was thoroughly embarrassed. I knew what good preaching was, and I knew what bad preaching was, and what had just happened was definitely bad! I wanted to leave immediately, but as a preacher's kid, I knew I had to stand in the lobby and let people come by and lie to me. Sure enough, some dear old ladies walked up to me and patted my hand, saying, "That was a wonderful, wonderful message." I did my best to smile as I thought to myself, "Did you have your hearing aid turned on?" Then the treasurer of the church came up and handed me an envelope. "Here's your honorarium," he said. Until that moment, I had no idea I was going to get paid for preaching, and honestly, I was so embarrassed that I didn't even want to take it, but he didn't give me a choice. As I got back in my car and drove home, I thought to myself, "You know, I thought I was supposed to like it. I didn't like it!" And that is how my preaching career began.

As I went off to college to begin training for the ministry, I did begin to grow. God began to place a burden on my heart for teenagers and outreach. Though I took some faith steps, I had not yet seen what I would call a full deliverance in preaching. I spent the summer after my freshman year back at home, working a job and doing some ministry at my dad's church. Toward the end of the summer, my dad stood before the church and announced, "Now, folks, before my son goes back to college, on a Sunday night in August, he is going to preach." It may surprise you, but I was actually kind of excited. I was growing in my walk with God, and I felt that I had made some progress in preaching. I still had no idea how to properly develop a message, but I spent some time "studying" Colossians 3 and wrote a few thoughts down on a piece of paper. To be honest, there wasn't much to it.

The big Sunday came, and my dad announced to the church again that I was going to preach that evening. I didn't need the reminder; I was already nervous! It's one thing to bore people that you'll never see again until you get to heaven. By that time, they will have forgiven you. It's another thing entirely to bore the hometown crowd! As we finished our Sunday afternoon dinner, I told my family, "I've got the basement. Please, nobody bother me."

I went down to the basement to get alone with God. For the first time in my life, I spent hours pleading with God. Most of it was not very sophisticated praying. I spent most of my time crying out, "God, You've got to do something. I can't do this. God, where are You? Please do something!" I didn't know much, but I knew enough to know this: I couldn't do it. Three hours passed by as I begged God to do something. You might wonder, "Preacher, why didn't you work on your outline?" Friend, the outline was on life support. Three hours could not have resuscitated it, and I knew it. My only hope was God. All I could do was constantly pray, "God, if You don't do something, I am done."

Around 5 o'clock, someone yelled down the stairs, "Hey, Jimmy, it's time to go!" Miserable, I walked up those wooden stairs, thinking, "This is terrible." The whole way to church, I was pleading, "God, You've got to do something. Don't You see I can't do this without You?" As the service began, I sat down in the chair beside my dad up on the platform. He sat calmly beside me, completely nonchalant, clearly not worried at all, while I sat there with my stomach tied in knots. From my seat on the platform, I could see that the auditorium was packed. At that time, it was nothing for the church to have five hundred people on a Sunday night. I think everybody came to see the preacher's kid go down in flames! After the song service, my dad calmly walked to the pulpit and introduced me. I'll never forget walking to that pulpit. I was still thinking, "God, I can't do this. God, please do something!" I opened my Bible, laid my sorry outline on the pulpit, and put my hands exactly where my dad always put his. Then I opened my mouth and began to preach. I hadn't gotten far into the message, when, all of a sudden, I had an overwhelming realization that I was not in that pulpit alone—God was there! I felt free. I stepped away from the pulpit to one side of the platform. There was an aisle right down the middle of the auditorium, and I began to preach to the crowd seated on one side. I would open my mouth and say something and then think, "Whoa! That was really good! Where did that come from? That's not in the outline!" After a few minutes I went over to the other side of the auditorium and started going after the crowd over there, and the same thing happened. I preached for 45 minutes and loved every minute of it! As I concluded my message, I gave an invitation. I saw people I'd known for most of my life coming down the aisle, some with tears. The altar was full. I learned something that night, something I now call **0/100**. I'd like to say that I've never had to relearn that lesson, but that wouldn't be true. However, that was the beginning of my journey in 0/100.

MY BEGINNING IN 0/100

You see, though I didn't know everything then that I know now, there were two things that were vividly clear to me. First, I couldn't do it. I had no ability to spiritually impact people's lives. Second, if God did not intervene, I was done. He was my only hope. I needed Him to do a miracle, and that is exactly what He did. But friend, that miracle would never have happened if I hadn't walked to the pulpit, opened my mouth, and begun to preach. I had to use physical strength that day, but I wasn't depending on my strength at all. It is the same for you. You won't know the miracle if you don't physically go to your next-door neighbor and invite them to church. You won't know the supernatural deliverance of God if you don't go to your wife and say, "Honey, I was wrong. Will you forgive me?" You won't experience God's stepping into your life, teenager, until you go to your parents and say, "God's been convicting me; I need to get something right with you." You won't know the miracle until you obey Jesus in dependence on His strength, not yours, to enable you to do what you could never do unless He enabled you to do it.

Friend, this is what 0/100 is all about—total surrender to the will of God and a total dependence on Jesus to enable you to do it. It's that simple. It's 0/100. It's His will, not mine. It's His strength, not mine. It's getting out of the boat when Jesus says, "Come!" and trusting Him to enable you to do what He has told you to do.

What boat do you need to get out of? Are you defeated in Bible reading/study and spending time with God? If that's your boat, take a step of faith. Get accountable—go to someone who loves you and say, "I've got to spend time with God every day. Keep me accountable." You might say, "My prayer life is almost non-existent; I hardly spend 5 or 10 minutes a day talking with God." Get out of the boat. Get on your knees and start crying out to God, trusting Jesus to give you wisdom to know what to pray for and to enable you to pray as long as He wants you to.

What about evangelism? Are you defeated, bound by unbelief and fear? Get out of the boat. Ask someone if they know where they will spend eternity. Trust Jesus to lead you to the ready harvest. Expect Him to enable you to win people to Jesus. Look to Him for strength to be bold with the gospel. He can enable you to go to your next-door neighbor. He can empower you to talk to your co-workers. He can enable you to do things you never thought you could do. How? By your taking that first step of faith and obedience, trusting Him to do through you what you know you cannot do. When the activity in your Christian life is totally God-dependent, then you will begin to know the reality of 0/100. Regardless of what your "boat" is, if you'll step out in dependence on Jesus, He will enable you to do what you thought you could never do. Will you get out of the boat?

Conclusion

"Complete weakness and dependence will always be the occasion for the Spirit of God to manifest His power."

Oswald Chambers

Conclusion

Do you remember the illustration of the Western Continental Divide that I gave in Chapter 1? It's just a simple line, but if two rain drops fall on opposite sides, though they land literally inches apart, their final destination is dramatically different. When it comes to the gospel, both for the sinner and the saint, there is a theological continental divide with equally dramatic consequences. Self-dependence lands you on one side, resulting in eternity in hell for the sinner, and frustration, pessimism, discouragement, and ultimate defeat for the saint. God-dependence lands you on the other side, resulting in eternal salvation for the sinner, and a life of joy and victory for the saint.

While a raindrop cannot decide which side of the Continental Divide it lands on, you **can** decide which side of God's divide you land on. It really is a question of the object of your faith: self, or God. That is the focus of 0/100. If you want to live on the "right side" of God's continental divide, you must take steps of obedience, depending 100% upon God and 0% on yourself. Anything else puts you on the "wrong side" of the continental divide.

This is the Gospel to the Saint. Yes, it's theology, but I trust you see now that it is far more than just theological truth to fill your head; it is paradigm-shifting reality that can change your life! It is practical truth that can be lived out in every step of your Christian life, no matter how impossible some steps may seem.

The last chapter closed with the simple question, "Will you get out of the boat?" Friend, the Christian life is impossible. You cannot do it in your own strength! And God knows that. That is why our loving

CONCLUSION

and all-powerful Savior says to you, "Come unto Me." Anything God wants you to do, He will enable you to do as you trust Him and obey. If you trust in your own strength in any measure, you will eventually be defeated. But if you live 0/100—totally surrendered to the will of God and totally dependent on Jesus to enable you—you, like Paul and like Peter, can have a Christian life of victory and fruitfulness! No matter what impossibility you are facing, Jesus invites you to "Come." **Will you get out of the boat?**

THEEGENERATION
WEBSITE

THEEGENERATION.ORG

THE BATTLE PLAN FOR VICTORY

THEEGENERATION.ORG/VICTORY

THEE GENERATION
PODCAST

THEEGENERATION.ORG/PODCAST

THEEGENERATION
YOUTH SUMMIT

Cola Clash

THEEGENERATION.ORG/SUMMIT